GABI'S FABULOUS FUNCTIONS

written by Caroline Karanja

illustrated by Ben Whitehouse

PICTURE WINDOW BOOKS
a capstone imprint

Meet our coding creatives!

This is Adi. Adi likes arts and crafts. She spends most of her time coloring, playing music, and making things. Whenever she sees something new, she wonders how it came to be. She likes to say, "I wonder . . ."

This is Gabi. Gabi loves to read, play outside, and take care of her dog, Charlie. She is always curious about how things work. Whenever she sees something that needs fixing, she tries to find the best way to improve it. She often says, "What if . . . ?"

Adi and Gabi make a great team!

Gabi and her mom are grocery shopping. They are buying ingredients that Gabi and Adi will need for some recipes. Recipes are instructions that lead to an end result: something delicious!

blueberries + strawberries + bananas = fruit salad

tomatoes + green peppers + lime juice + cilantro = salsa

Today is Gabi's father's birthday. Gabi wants to make him breakfast. Adi has come over to help.

Gabi's mom had to go to work. Before she left, she prepared the ingredients for fruit salad and breakfast tostadas.

"Let's start with the fruit salad," Adi says. "It's the easiest."

"Here's what we need," Gabi says, reading the recipe. "Blueberries, strawberries . . ."

"Mixing ingredients to make something new is like a function in computer programming," Adi says. "When you ask for a cookie, you don't say, 'Please pass the eggs and flour and sugar and butter and chocolate chips.' You just say, 'Pass the cookies, please!'"

"A function is like a recipe for a computer!" Gabi says. "It tells the computer that when you say 'cookie,' what you really mean is: eggs, flour, sugar, butter, and chocolate chips all mixed and baked into circle shapes."

Functions

A function is a block of code that performs a certain task. It tells a computer what you need it to do, without having to explain every step. Functions help programmers avoid having to repeat the same actions over and over. If you need to do a task again and again, you can create a function that works as a shortcut. Functions have an input (like the ingredients) and an output (like the cookie).

"Instead of fruit salad, how about if we make a parfait?" Adi suggests.

"What's a parfait?" Gabi asks.

"It's made with yogurt, berries, and granola. Since we already have berries, we just need some yogurt and granola," Adi says.

Gabi checks the refrigerator. "We have those."

"Great!" Adi says. She puts some yogurt in a bowl and adds some berries.

Then Gabi adds a sprinkle of granola. "All done!"

Gabi picks up the tostada recipe. "So if recipes are like functions, the input for this would be: refried beans, grated cheese, avocado, lettuce, salsa, and a corn tortilla," she says.

Adi and Gabi put together the tostada using the ingredients Gabi's mother prepared.

"And the output is the tostada!" Adi cheers. "Now we just need to warm it up."

"Let's make some more parfaits," Gabi says. "What if we make a function factory? A parfait function factory!"

The girls make a sign that says *input*.
They put it next to the ingredients sitting
on the counter: yogurt, berries, and granola.
Then they make a sign that says *output* for
the finished parfaits.

Between the two signs, they set up a box
that says *function*.

"When we input the ingredients, our output will be a parfait!" Gabi says.

Gabi's dad comes into the kitchen.

"Happy birthday!" Gabi and Adi call out.

"We used functions to make your breakfast," Gabi explains.

"Let's show your dad our parfait function factory!" Adi says.

"OK, I'll be the computer," Gabi says. She stands behind the box so that her dad can't see what she's doing. "Input, please!" she says to Adi.

Adi hands her the yogurt,
berries, and granola. Behind
the box, Gabi quickly mixes the
ingredients into a fancy glass
to make a parfait. Then she sets
the finished parfait next to the
output sign.

Ding! goes the toaster oven.
"Now your tostada is ready too!"
Gabi says. She carefully puts it on a
plate and gives it to her dad. Adi hands
him his parfait.

Gabi's dad dips a spoon into the parfait and takes a bite. "Well, this is the most delicious 'output' I've ever had!" he says. "Good coding—and cooking—girls!"

Which function makes the perfect pizza?

Adi and Gabi decide to make a pizza for lunch. The ingredients—or input—for their pizza are cheese, sauce, dough, and pepperoni. Just like code blocks in a function, ingredients need to go in a certain order to get the right result. Which row shows the correct order to get the right results for a pizza?

Glossary

code—one or more rules or commands to be carried out by a computer

code block—a set of code that is grouped together

computer—an electronic machine that can store and work with large amounts of information

function—a set of steps or instructions that together create a specific result

input—a command that is entered

output—the result of a specific set of commands and steps being entered

programmer—a person who writes code that can be run by a machine

task—a piece of work that needs to be done

Think in Code!

- Think of your favorite game. Can you write the function or set of instructions for playing the game?

- Come up with a function to make your favorite sandwich. Don't forget to include all the inputs—or your output won't come out right!

- See how many functions you can find in your day. Did you make a craft? Make a bowl of cereal? Those are functions! What other functions can you think of?

About the Author

Caroline Karanja is a developer and designer who is on a mission to increase accessibility and sustainability through technology. She enjoys figuring out how things work and sharing this knowledge with others. She lives in Minneapolis.

This book is dedicated to Anaïs
for your friendship and encouragement —C. K.

Picture Window Books are published by Capstone
1710 Roe Crest Drive, North Mankato, Minnesota 56003
www.mycapstone.com

Library of Congress Cataloging-in-Publication data is available on the Library of Congress website.

978-1-5158-3444-1 (paper over board)
978-1-5158-2743-6 (library hardcover)
978-1-5158-2747-4 (paperback)
978-1-5158-2751-1 (eBook PDF)

Summary: Two friends explore how functions used in computer programming can
also be used in their everyday lives—especially in the kitchen!

Editor: Kristen Mohn
Designer: Kay Fraser
Design Element: Shutterstock/Arcady

Printed and bound in the United States of America.
PA021